18x 12/14 LT 6/14

18x 12/14 LT 6/14

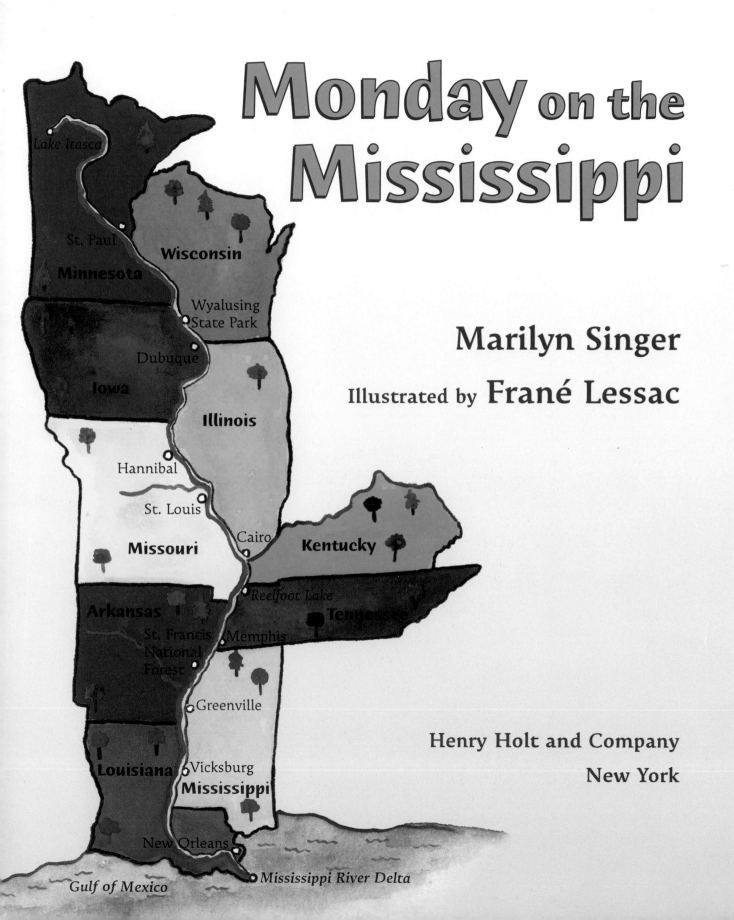

Monday on the Mississippi

Marilyn Singer

Illustrated by Frané Lessac

Henry Holt and Company

New York

Map labels: Lake Itasca, St. Paul, Minnesota, Wisconsin, Wyalusing State Park, Dubuque, Iowa, Illinois, Hannibal, St. Louis, Missouri, Cairo, Kentucky, Reelfoot Lake, Arkansas, Tennessee, St. Francis National Forest, Memphis, Greenville, Louisiana, Vicksburg, Mississippi, New Orleans, Gulf of Mexico, Mississippi River Delta

The map in the illustration reads:

Manitoba, Canada

Ontario, Canada

North Dakota

Mississippi River

Lake Superior

LAKE ITASCA

South Dakota

St. Paul

Wisconsin

MINNESOTA

Iowa

Monday on the Mississippi

Lake Itasca, Minnesota

A little lake among so many lakes.
A little stream among so many streams.
A little girl wiggles her toes
in the shallow water and wonders,
How long before we're big and strong, little Mississippi?
How many miles? How many days?

Monday on the Mississippi

St. Paul, Minnesota

Each pilot at the wheel,
each lockman at the gates,
each deckhand and dockhand,
all take up the chant:
Wheat barge, corn barge, salt barge—
tow, push 'em down the river.
Scrap barge, sand barge, coal barge—
go, push 'em down the river.
Water's thrashing. Watch—no crashing!
Moline, Commerce, Baton Rouge.
Push 'em down the river!

Lake Superior
Michigan
WISCONSIN
Mississippi River
Minnesota
Wyalusing State Park
Iowa
Madison
Lake Michigan
Dubuque
Illinois

Tuesday on the Mississippi

Wyalusing State Park, Wisconsin

The Great Bear watches over the Mississippi.
It is younger than the river.
It is older than the river's name.
Four hikers wonder how, when, why
those long-gone people
built it here of earth and stones.
Their children stand wide-eyed on the trail,
listening for its footsteps, hearing its ancient growl.

Tuesday on the Mississippi

Dubuque, Iowa

On the levee the old men swap stories
of the bad old days when sharks
rode the riverboats to skin the fools
of money, jewels, teams of mules,
houses, and entire farms,
taking imaginary bets on whose granddad
was the better gambler
and whose granddad lost the most.

Wednesday on the Mississippi

Hannibal, Missouri

On the Fourth of July, in spattered overalls,
ten boys from every state along the Mississippi
race to paint Tom Sawyer's fence and win a prize.

Later that day, up on Cardiff Hill,
looking down at the silent water,
dreaming of books and baseball,
rafts and jumping frogs,
one of them will hear a ghost's
rough voice on the breeze:
"Steamboat a-comin'. Get on board."
He will tip his tattered hat
to a time that once was,
to a river that will always be.

Wednesday on the Mississippi

St. Louis, Missouri

Pouring out of the stadium, they're still talking
about how bottom of the ninth he smacked that,
whacked that fastball so hard
it must've sailed two blocks through the Arch
right into the river,
where it's teaching "Take Me Out to the Ball Game"
to the gulls and fishes
all the way down to the Delta.

ILLINOIS

Wisconsin

Dubuque

Iowa

Lake
Michigan

Indiana

Springfield

Mississippi River

Hannibal

St. Louis

Ohio River

Missouri

CAIRO

Kentucky

Thursday on the Mississippi

Cairo, Illinois

The pilot learned to fly
so she could see from the sky
blue water, brown water, all around water.
Water from one hundred thousand lakes,
rivers, streams joining here—
where the great Ohio
meets the mighty "Mississippi,"
a word the eager young copilot
has just now learned to spell.

Thursday on the Mississippi

Reelfoot Lake, Kentucky-Tennessee Border

"Earthquake!" the cousins shout, rocking the canoe,
trying to scare the girls with something
that happened two hundred years ago,
when the crazed river ran backward for three whole days
and threw up this here lake the boys think
will be just right for tossing in
those trouble-making, double-talking twins.

Ohio

Indiana

Illinois

St.
Louis

Mississippi River

Ohio River

Cairo

Kentucky

Missouri

Virginia

Reelfoot Lake

★ Nashville

North
Carolina

Arkansas

TENNESSEE

MEMPHIS

St. Francis
National
Forest

Mississippi River

South
Carolina

Mississippi

Alabama

Georgia

Friday on the Mississippi

Memphis, Tennessee

At Mud Island, where their brothers admire
the perfect miniature model of the Mississippi—
its tiny towns, its little twists and turns—
two sisters want to sit quietly by the real thing,
listening for Martin Luther, B.B., Elvis,
and all the others that would've been,
should've been,
or never could've been.
They want to sit and hear the river that rings
with the voices of Kings.

The map shows:

Missouri

Tennessee

Arkansas River

Mississippi River

ST. FRANCIS
NATIONAL
FOREST

Memphis

Oklahoma

Little Rock

ARKANSAS

Mississippi

Texas

Mississippi River

Greenville

Louisiana

Friday on the Mississippi

St. Francis National Forest, Arkansas

July rice keeps growing in the paddies,
cotton keeps growing in the fields,
black ducks keep floating on the water.
White-tailed deer keep hiding in the woods,
gators keep lying in the swamp grass,
skeeters keep biting folks' skin.

And that same stubborn catfish keeps swimming
up and down the river,
bristling his whiskers to his ten-years-long summer song:
"You can't catch me.
No, sir. You will NEVER catch me."

St. Francis
National
Forest

Memphis Tennessee

Arkansas River

MISSISSIPPI

Arkansas

GREENVILLE

Vicksburg

Jackson

Mississippi River

Alabama

Louisiana

New Orleans Gulf of Mexico

DELTA QUEEN

Saturday on the Mississippi

Greenville, Mississippi

Under this bridge folks from over Alabama way,
down from Delaware and even Maine
think they'll see nothin' but an old brown river
moving nice and lazy.
They don't know how fast and deep it runs.
They have never seen that river go crazy
like that once-upon-a-time
when all the houses took a ride
on the Mississippi Ocean more than fifty miles wide.

Memphis Tennessee

St. Francis
National
Forest

Arkansas River

Arkansas

MISSISSIPPI

Greenville

VICKSBURG

Louisiana

Jackson

Alabama

Mississippi River

New Orleans

Gulf of Mexico

Saturday on the Mississippi

Vicksburg, Mississippi

The guide is telling a tale dark as the gathering clouds:
"1863. North and South. Whoever held this river
was sure to win the war."
Thunder booms like cannonfire.
The visitors jump, then watch wide-eyed
as the wind grabs the guide's favorite hat
and tosses it into the water.
The Mississippi waves it once like a tattered flag,
then swallows it whole.

Sunday on the Mississippi

New Orleans, Louisiana

Early Sunday morning,
when even the Mississippi seems too tired to roll,
a single saxophone player swaying on the Esplanade
wails the river's long story,
black-coffee bitter, warm-beignet sweet,
to anyone awake enough to listen.

LOUISIANA

Mississippi

Vicksburg

Mississippi River

Texas

Baton Rouge

New Orleans

Gulf of Mexico

MISSISSIPPI
RIVER DELTA

Sunday on the Mississippi

Mississippi River Delta, Louisiana

A broad channel among so many channels.
A small boat among such giant ships.
A little boy on the deck watches the brown pelicans
trailing in the wake and wonders,
Will I ever see where you start, big Mississippi?
Will I ever tell where you end
and the wide, wide sea begins?

About the Mississippi

Big Muddy. Old Man River. The Father of Waters. These are all nicknames for the Mississippi—an Ojibwe word meaning "great river." It begins as a small stream at Lake Itasca, Minnesota, and flows over 2,300 miles through ten states to the Gulf of Mexico. Rivers from thirty-one states in all eventually drain into it. The Mississippi is not the longest river in North America; one of its tributaries, the Missouri, is. But it is the most famous—a river of legends, songs, poems, and stories.

In the 1800s, the well-known writer Mark Twain grew up alongside the river in Hannibal, Missouri. He made the Mississippi famous by celebrating it in many of his books. Now each summer Hannibal celebrates Mark Twain and his characters during National Tom Sawyer Days.

Besides being an author, Twain was once a steamboat pilot. Steamboats, gambling boats, tows, all kinds of crafts, have traveled up and down the Mississippi, delivering cargo and offering entertainment and transportation for passengers. Today, the steamboats are mostly gone, except as tourist attractions. But the tows are very much in use. Some of them can push more than thirty barges at a time. To make the Mississippi easier for the tows and other commercial traffic to navigate, engineers have built a system of locks and dams on the upper river. They have also built levees and created channels to control flooding. But even with all the attempts to restrain the river, it can still be unpredictable and dangerous.

The river's route travels through a landscape rich in variety and history. Up north it runs between high wooded bluffs, some topped with

burial and ceremonial mounds, several of which are shaped like animals. These mounds were built by Native American people who lived there long ago, probably to celebrate the connection of people and the natural world. As it flows south, it passes through small towns, farmlands, swamps, bayous, and big cities: Minneapolis/St. Paul; St. Louis, where the Gateway Arch stands; Memphis, where musicians Elvis Presley and B. B. King lived and civil rights leader Martin Luther King Jr. died; and New Orleans.

Its path is marked by sites of bloody massacres and Civil War battles; by disasters such as the 1927 flood, which destroyed many homes and farms in Greenville, Mississippi, and way beyond; and the New Madrid, Missouri, earthquakes of 1811–12, when the river ran backward and created Reelfoot Lake at the border of Kentucky and Tennessee. It flows past magnificent parks and preserves, factories, museums, poor shacks, and great mansions. On its shores you'll find all kinds of plants and animals and people of many races and nationalities who've come to live by the Great River Road.

Today the Mississippi faces problems such as pollution and loss of wildlife habitat—problems that many people are working to solve. But still it teems with life and vitality. It is an ever-changing place where bald eagles fish in winter, kids fish in summer, and folks hold festivals, make music, build ballparks, picnic, and dream of the river that was and the river that will be.

To Oggi, Poodle of the Mississippi —M. S.

For Luke . . . wishing you a life full of travel and adventure —F. L.

Acknowledgments

Thanks to Paul C. Artman Jr., former mayor of Greenville, Mississippi; Stacey Carpenter; Chuck Galey; David Haggard; Scott D. Johnson; Dara Kiese; Kevin and Amy Knickerbocker; Scott Miller; Lyn Miller-Lachmann; Laura Nagel; Tracy L. Powers; Beverly Slapin; John Smith; Marilyn Snyder; Nancy Thomas; Sarah Thomson; Robert Weih; Peter H. Yaukey—and especially to Steve Aronson, for being a great traveling partner; Joe Angert and Pat Middleton, for their expert critiques; Frané Lessac, for her fabulous art; and Christy Ottaviano, Adriane Frye, and the folks at Holt, for helping this book be. —M. S.

With special thanks to May Gibbs Children's Literature Trust Canberra; Jil Belle Hales, co-captain and navigator, Memphis to New Orleans; Scott D. Johnson, Wyalusing State Park, Wisconsin; Denise Vondron, Mississippi River Museum, Dubuque, Iowa; Bryan Hammoch, Hannibal Jaycees, Hannibal, Missouri; Bonnie Koop, Audubon Society, Great River Birding Trail; Maru L. Wood, St. Francis National Forest, Arkansas. —F. L.

Artist supported by ArtsWA in association with the Lotteries Commission to travel down the Mississippi River.

Henry Holt and Company, LLC, *Publishers since 1866*, 115 West 18th Street, New York, New York 10011
www.henryholt.com

Henry Holt is a registered trademark of Henry Holt and Company, LLC
Text copyright © 2005 by Marilyn Singer. Illustrations copyright © 2005 by Frané Lessac
All rights reserved. Distributed in Canada by H. B. Fenn and Company Ltd.

Library of Congress Cataloging-in-Publication Data
Singer, Marilyn. Monday on the Mississippi / by Marilyn Singer; illustrated by Frané Lessac.—1st ed.   p.   cm.
Summary: Describes scenes along the Mississippi River over the course of a week, beginning in Minnesota when it is a tiny stream and going all the way to the gulf coast of Louisiana. Includes a section of historical information about the river.
ISBN-13: 978-0-8050-7208-2
ISBN-10: 0-8050-7208-X
[1. Mississippi River—Fiction.] I. Lessac, Frané, ill. II. Title.   PZ7.S6172Mo 2005   [Fic]—dc22   2004009198
First Edition—2005 / Designed by Donna Mark / The artist used gouache on paper to create the illustrations for this book.
Printed in the United States of America on acid-free paper. ∞
10 9 8 7 6 5 4 3 2 1